A Bible Study Program
Using the Sunday Lectionary

A Bible Study Program
Using the Sunday Lectionary

————————

Taking your study group to the next level

Fr. Robert R Beck
robert.beck@loras.edu

RESOURCE *Publications* • Eugene, Oregon

A BIBLE STUDY PROGRAM USING THE SUNDAY LECTIONARY
Taking Your Bible Study Group to the Next Level

Resource Publications
An Imprint of Wipf and Stock Publishers
199 W. 8th Ave., Suite 3
Eugene, OR 97401

www.wipfandstock.com

ISBN 13: 978-1-62564-455-8

Manufactured in the U.S.A.

Contents

Introduction   7

I. Reading: The World-of-the-Text   9

Ch 1. What do our ears notice? Reading the text aloud   11

Ch. 2. What is the passage saying? The text as statement   13

Ch. 3. What is being emphasized? Key words and terms   15

Ch. 4. What engages our imagination? Images, metaphors, symbols   17

Ch. 5. What kind of writing is this? Literary forms and genres   19

Ch. 6. What is strange? Special words and terms   23

Ch. 7. Who is speaking in the passage? Implied voices and hearers   25

II. Background and Context: The World-Behind-the-Text   27

Ch. 8. What do the experts say? The commentaries   29

Ch. 9. What was happening when the passage was written? Historical setting   31

Ch. 10. Why was the passage written? The social location of the writer   37

Ch. 11. Who is being quoted? Using cross-references   39

III. Community of Believers: The World-in-Front-of-the-Text   43

Ch. 12. Why does it matter? Application; social location of the reader   45

Ch. 13. The Lectionary: Seasons   49

Ch. 14. The Lectionary: Cycles   53

Appendix 1: Sample texts   59

Appendix 2: List of examples from the Lectionary   63

Selected Bibliography   65

Introduction

To be clear about it, this is a Bible study method and not a program for Bible sharing or biblical prayer. The intent here is to hold off on devotional activity in order to leave room for study. The underlying assumption is that increased knowledge of the Bible will aid in biblical devotion. While biblical prayer is encouraged, the hope is that those using this method will explore the text at least to learning something new for each session.

The method is divided into two parts, corresponding to the world-of-the-text itself ("Reading") and the world-behind-the-text ("Background and Context"— Sandra Schneiders, *The Revelatory Text*, introduces these categories into biblical reading.). The first of these consists of a number of strategies for a close reading of the text. The assumption is that the Bible, written in human language, uses the literary forms and genres of human culture in which that language is always found. Another way to say this: the word of God comes to us in the form of literature. As a collection of different kinds of literary forms and genres, these provide criteria for how the different books are to be read. Also, since we are accustomed to relying on what others have to say about the biblical texts, this attention to assistance in reading it for oneself might be welcomed.

The second section, devoted to the world-behind-the-text, looks at the world in which the biblical books were written. This is where the biblical aids such as commentaries, atlases, and biblical concordances enter in. For these purposes the present method uses the Catholic Study Bible, which includes a section of Reading Guides, cross-referenced with the Bible itself. While a more complete treatment of this dimension would involve stand-alone commentaries and other aids, the Reading Guides provide an adequate resource for our purposes. Other resources are to be added as needed.

Along with the world-of-the-text and the world-behind-the-text, there is the world-in-front-of-the-text ("The Community of Believers"), which is where we the readers are to be found. This is the concern of the Part III. Unlike many of the popular evangelical Bible study approaches which are directed toward isolated individual believers, this method presupposes a believing community. For this reason the method is based on the Sunday lectionary readings. Not only does it evoke the universal church gathered weekly in prayer, but also the study program would hope to make that weekly experience more fruitful. The Sunday lectionary provides an effective program for Bible study, insofar as it cycles through much of the Bible in its three-year course. However, many of the selections are much too brief for real comprehension, a problem that a study program with its more expansive look at the texts will help to resolve.

N.B., Reference to the Lectionary is by Week-Season-Cycle. Thus (1 Adv A) *is to be read as the First Sunday of Advent, Cycle A.*

How to use this book

This book can be considered a tool kit for Bible study groups. The ideas are arranged in a sequence set up for learning, from more familiar to less so. In the initial reading, this might be the best sequence.

But this is not the best way for them to be used. Rather, as in any tool kit, they are to be called upon when they fit the task. The seven chapters in the first part offer different approaches for coming to terms with the text in front of us. Different texts may call for different strategies. Some are useful most of the time. Others not so often, but they are included so that they will be available when needed.

The next seven chapters go beyond the text in front of us to call upon external aids and Bible helps. These are described briefly, since the helps themselves will provide the assistance needed. However, the same principle holds: use them whenever it promises to help; there is no need to make in every session an exhaustive use of the possibilities given here.

Getting started

After surveying the various chapters in this book, there still remains the question of putting them into practice. How to begin? How can we know which approach will best serve our purposes for any particular study session? Like any case of learning a new procedure, the best and most secure mastery comes through practice. But here are a few things to keep in mind.

Each chapter includes sample questions to ask concerning the biblical passage. These questions may help to get us started. At the same time, they might suggest whether or not the particular chapter applies to this passage.

Some of the strategies gathered below can apply to any text, and might be included in a regular program of study. For example, reading the passages aloud (ch. 1) or clarifying what statements are being made (ch. 2) might be useful for starting explorations. On the other hand, some do not apply everywhere. Nevertheless, where they do they can be surprisingly helpful. For instance, poetic lines can benefit from awareness of the literary form of parallelism (ch. 5), or the use of images (ch. 4). Understanding passages from the prophetic writing might benefit from an awareness of the voices speaking in the text (ch. 7).

The program is designed to allow a reader to grow in understanding the biblical texts. The beauty and art of much biblical writing will gradually unfold itself to the reader. But the realization that there are aspects (as in the examples given here) that we may never have suspected ought not to discourage us. Even when we are beginning on this exploration we will frequently find much to surprise us. Be assured, the surprises never stop coming, no matter how often or long you follow this or any program of Bible study.

Part I. Reading: The World-of-the-Text

The following pages offer a program for studying the Bible using the Sunday lectionary. It also uses as a primary resource the *Catholic Study Bible*. The program consists of a series of how-to steps. As noted earlier, these are arranged in the order of learning, from most familiar to least. But they are conceived as a "tool kit" to be used as needed, and not necessarily in the particular order in which they are presented. The steps consist of a series of questions in two sections. Each set of questions leads into a short explanation of the issues they introduce.

The first section, following here, concerns the biblical text itself. The second section looks at the world behind the text, with the authors and their settings, as well as the world in front of the text, where we, the readers, interpret the word for our own situations. Third party commentaries are not ignored, but because the objective of the program is to assist the reader in working with the biblical text directly, they are deferred to a later moment when they can act as confirmation of the reader's own efforts.

The questions presuppose that biblical writing is literary. Without questioning in the least the Bible's status as God's word, it makes the assumption that this word comes to us as artful literature. As such, it invites study using literary tools of interpretation.

Driving a car: An Example of the Complexity of a Common Practice

The method seems more complex than it is. An example of this phenomenon is driving a car. Driver's training covers only the basics, belabored as it is. Experience covers the other 90%.

> The basic, though complex, mechanical art of simply operating a vehicle
> The safety part: buckling up, watching the kids, their car seat, etc.
> The auto maintenance part: paying attention to the machine's needs
> The efficiency part: planning one's route, whether grocery store or vacation
> The defensive driving part: anticipating what other drivers are going to do
> The weather and road conditions part: gravel, winter driving, potholes, etc.

With practice and experience, all of these blend into a single act. The individual parts no longer preoccupy a driver in the fragmented way they do during driver's training. So it can be with these study methods.

Ch 1. What do our ears notice? *Reading the text aloud*

Read the liturgical selections through thoughtfully and prayerfully.

Questions:

What is the main point as you hear it?
What is unexpected or surprising?

The importance of reading aloud:

You are invited to read through the entire set of readings at the start. Different members of the group can take different readings. Beginning a session with reading the passages aloud offers distinct benefits. If done carefully and prayerfully, it can set the tone and place the group in a suitable frame of mind. Also, in this way it duplicates and evokes the liturgical experience in church, reminding us that this is the community in prayer.

In addition, it slows down our attention, keeping us from skimming and skipping over parts that might be worth noticing. Also, it is true that some people learn better with their ears than their eyes.

Example: Matthew 1:18-25 — Joseph's Dream (4 Adv A)

Read through the passage aloud. Jot down something you heard this time, but haven't noticed before. Also write down what you expected to hear, but did not. Finally, you might write down what you consider to be the main point of the passage. If you are doing this in a group, discuss. If you are doing this alone, reflect on your results and capture your thoughts in writing.

Eventually, this practice will become a habit, and it will not be necessary to write down the findings. But it can always stand in reserve, as something to rely upon if needed.

For further exploration:

In chapter 7, below, we will be looking at the presence of different voices in readings. It can be instructive to read such passages aloud with more than one reader, simulating the voices in the text.

Ch. 2. What is the passage saying? *The text as statement*

In studying the details of the passage we are engaged in a "close reading." There are many values to such a procedure. For familiar passages it allows a fresh look. In some cases, this means overcoming previous ideas of what the passage means. For unfamiliar passages it allows a means of access, which otherwise can be a problem.

Questions to ask:

What are the main parts of the passage?
How do they relate to one another?
How would you paraphrase the passage?

Does the lectionary leave something out?

What in the passage supports your impressions?

Throughout this method we want to support our interpretations with features of the text itself—"text facts." If we consistently support our interpretations in this way we are less likely to get mired in our preconceptions. We find a way to move beyond our first impressions, or see beyond our favorite themes, which can get in the way of seeing what the text is saying. It also helps to keep us from making things up about the text.

What do we look for in this step? Paying attention to basic grammar is important. Having the correct grammatical terminology is not as important as being aware of how the grammar, or sense of the passage, is working. Pay attention to punctuation. Determine, for example, how many sentences are in the passage. How do they relate? How do they add up to a statement of some sort? Some items to be aware of are these:

- **Patterns**: A common sentence pattern is "if/then." It is often found in prophetic passages, and Paul's letters. In some cases, the explicit terms "if" and "then" are not expressed, but the meaning is there. There are other ways that parts of a sentence relate. Another common pattern is "question/answer." This may be enough to let you discover your own. Sometimes sentences of a certain style are repeated to form a pattern. In general, watch for patterns that shape a passage.

- **Repetition**: A common feature of biblical writing is repetition of a key sentence, phrase or term. Repetition is used to draw comparisons between sections, to introduce or conclude comparable passages, or to bracket a passage with a theme. Repetition is an important component in any formal pattern in the text.

- **Quotations**: A frequent pattern, especially in prophetic speech, is that of a narrator introducing a speaker. The interplay between narrative and quoted voices invites a reader's attention. (For an extended version of this, see Ch. 7, below.)

- **Parallelism**: A key feature of biblical poetry is "parallelism"—a form of repetition that includes entire lines (see chapter 5). Identifying poetic parallelism will assist in sorting out the grammatical sense of a passage.

> *Example*:
>
> Isaiah 49:14-15   (8 Ord A)
>
> Can a mother forget her infant?
> Zion said, "The LORD has forsaken me;
> my LORD has forgotten me."
>
> Can a mother forget her infant,
> be without tenderness for the child of her womb?
>
> Even should she forget,
> I will never forget you.

In this example we see the following features:

- **The question/answer pattern** provides the basic form. The entire passage can be described in a few assertions: twice a question is asked, and twice it is answered.

- **Repetition**: the question/answer pattern occurs twice. This invites us to make a comparison. Concerning the question, the second time it is amplified, perhaps for rhetorical reasons. The two answers form a distinct contrast. First, Zion (Jerusalem) answers. The second answerer is not identified, but we understand it is God. The negative view of the first answer is reversed by the second answer.

  NB: Note how we have come to the point where we can see that the question/answer pattern is echoed in the two exchanges. The first, with Zion's answer, acts like a question that the second, the Lord's different answer, acts like a response to Zion's despair.

- **Parallelism**: the entire passage is cast in poetic parallelism. This is noticeably true of the two questions, in regard to each other. In addition, the second time the question is uttered it generates a second line with parallel meaning. The two answers are parallel in an antithetical contrast. (See Ch. 5, below.)

  Features of the passage explored in later chapters:
Key words: mother, forget	(Ch. 3)
Imagery: mother/child	(Ch. 4)
Implied voices: Zion/Lord	(Ch. 7)

For further exploration:

Isaiah 58:7-10	(5 Ord A)	if / then
Isaiah 43:16-21	(5 Lent C)	parts, quotation
1 Corinthians 2:1-5	(5 Ord A)	parts, repetitions, oppositions

Ch. 3. What is being emphasized? *Key words and terms*

A feature of most writing, including biblical writing, is the use of key terms and phrases. We are familiar with topic sentences in paragraphs, for example. Identifying these key terms in a passage can focus our understanding, and often point the way to the writer's intention.

Questions to ask:

What terms or phrases are repeated?
Are there prominent contrasts or opposed terms in the passage?
Are these dictionary contrasts, or do they derive from the author's thinking?
Can they be organized?

Here are some of the ways to explore key terms in seeking the meaning of biblical texts.

- **Dominant position**: While topic sentences are generally found at the beginning of a paragraph, the location of a phrase or term that carries special weight may appear elsewhere, for instance, in a concluding position.

- **Repetition**: Typically, repetition of a term indicates its special status. In the previous chapter repetition was discussed as a guide to the formal features of a passage. Here it is viewed in another aspect—its ability to guide us to emphasized terms and phrases. The same strategies of repetition apply here—framing sections, similar beginnings or endings—but now we are interested in how they point to key ideas.

- **Oppositions**: An additional feature of repetition is its ability to set up oppositions in the text. These often are a key to its meaning. What to watch for in this case are:
  - making comparisons between parts.
  - making a point by contrast;
  - structuring a narrative by contrasts or tensions;
  - illustrating values.

Examples of the use of Repetition:

Luke 15: 11-32, The Prodigal Son parable (24 Ord C): The story of the younger son and the story of the older son each ends with the father's remarks (15:24, 32): "Let us celebrate and rejoice for this son of mine (your brother) was dead, and has come to life again; he was lost and has been found." This repetition not only states the theme of the story, but by concluding the account of each brother, invites us to compare them.

Exodus 22:20-26, The Cry of the Poor, (30 Ord A), see Appendix 1, example 4: The repeated sequence of vv. 20-23, 24-26 invites us to consider the concluding contrast between the God's wrath (v. 23) and compassion (v. 26).

An example of use of oppositions:

Galatians 5:1, 13-18 (13 Ord C): A useful tool in reading the letters of Paul is alertness to his opposed terms. A good example is in Galatians 5, where we find opposing terms such as freedom/slavery, Spirit/flesh, law/love, etc. (See example 5, Appendix 1). Notice that most of the opposed terms come from Paul's thought, and are not simply dictionary contrasts (such as hot/cold, or love/hate). Paying attention to Paul's terminology can be a clue to his thinking.

By the way, oppositional terms is a frequent feature of many kinds of writing, and not only Paul's letters.

For further exploration:

A specialized form of comparison in Gospel study is reviewing parallels among the three Synoptic Gospels, Matthew, Mark, and Luke. Books like Throckmorton's *Gospel Parallels* (see bibliography) are designed for such study. By comparing what Gospels have added, omitted, or altered allows us to gain an understanding of the different writers' emphases and interests.

Ch. 4. What engages our imagination? *Images, metaphors, symbols*

A feature of biblical writing often ignored in our usual rush to meaning is its use of imagery. Like key terms, images also have the ability to condense the meaning of a passage in a small space. Images are especially useful in understanding poetry. Attention to the use of images also can assist in reading Paul's letters.

Questions to ask:

Are certain images repeated?
Are there clusters of related images?

Are images used in comparisons (metaphors)?
What is being compared?

Is there an image prominent enough to qualify as a primary image, a symbol?
If so, what might it symbolize?

For the sake of convenience, we can consider images under three headings: *images proper, metaphors,* and *symbols.*

- **Images** relate to our senses—they are mental representations of sensory input. Senses are more than visual, and images are as well (though visual images predominate). Vivid language is rich in images, and often uses these images to make its points. Biblical authors do the same.

- **Metaphors** are images used in comparisons. Frequently metaphors take the place of straightforward language. One reason is that it is more difficult to be completely explicit. Parables are narrative metaphors: where a metaphor stands for an idea, the parable's story stands for the Kingdom.

- **Symbols**, for our purposes, can be thought of as images that dominate the passages in which they are found. The symbol typically stands for the entire passage. Images can be said to organize certain passages, just as they can organize certain liturgies.

A sensitivity to the use of images will offer another way to appreciate the connections among the readings of a given Sunday, as well. For instance, in the 24th Sunday of Ordinary Time, Cycle C, the Golden Calf of Exodus 32 contrasts with the Fatted Calf of the Prodigal Son parable in Luke 15.

Example:

Isa 43:16-21 (5 Lent C)

Thus says the LORD,
who opens a way in the sea,
a path in the mighty waters,
Who leads out chariots and horsemen,
a powerful army,
Till they lie prostrate together, never to rise,
snuffed out, quenched like a wick.

Remember not the events of the past,
the things of long ago consider not;
See, I am doing something new!
Now it springs forth, do you not perceive it?
In the wilderness I make a way,
in the wasteland, rivers.
Wild beasts honor me,
jackals and ostriches,
For I put water in the wilderness
and rivers in the wasteland
for my chosen people to drink,
The people whom I formed for myself,
that they might recount my praise.

The passage illustrates how imagery can sort out a text. In the first part of the passage the images are taken from the story of the Exodus, and Israel's crossing of the Red (Reed) Sea. In the second part of the passage the images evoke the Arabian desert and the return from exile in Babylon. Note how the imagery here reverses that of the sea crossing. Instead of a dry path through the sea it describes a well-watered path through the arid desert.

For further exploration:

In chapter 7 we will consider the various voices that are in the text. Notice that here the speaker changes after the seventh line. The first part introduces the main speaker, who is God.

Ch. 5. What kind of writing is this? *Literary forms and genres*

All writing follows some kind of form. The classes of literary forms are commonly called genres and sub-genres. In biblical commentaries they are often called literary forms. Though frequently changing, forms and genres are determined by the culture in which the writer lives. Awareness of the form allows us to interpret a text correctly. It is what helps us find books in bookstores and make our way through newspapers. We know the difference between a news report and an editorial, and adjust our expectations accordingly.

Questions to ask:

What kind of writing is this?
What in the text itself shows this?

What is the purpose of this kind of writing?
If poetry, how does it use parallelism?

When we share a culture with a writer, this part of reading largely goes unnoticed. But when we do not share the writer's culture, as is the case with biblical texts, we need to be more conscious of the literary forms. Our situation might be compared to visiting a foreign country. When we do this it is usually a good idea to prepare ourselves by learning about the customs of the place. So it is with the Bible, which was written in the Middle East some 20 to 25 centuries ago.

The introductions to the various biblical books, such as those found in the Catholic Study Bible, typically identify the kind of writing involved, along with some tips on reading. Here are some general descriptions of some main biblical forms.

Some (but certainly not all) Old Testament forms:

- **Psalm**: Psalms are the words to hymns used in the temple liturgy. Two basic kinds are psalms of praise and psalms of lament. Secondary types are psalms of thanksgiving and psalms of confidence. In these, watch for three parts—a call to prayer; a central part that gives reasons for the praise or lament; a conclusion that returns to opening sentiments (or, in the case of laments and psalms of confidence, words of praise). Specialized forms that will be identified in your Bible are royal, wisdom, didactic, and enthronement psalms. (For examples of psalms of praise see Pss 8, 19, 29. For examples of psalms of lament, see Pss. 5, 6, 7.)

- **Prophetic Oracle**: The prophets employed a number of forms, but underlying them all was the prophetic oracle. These separate into two basic forms—psalms of judgment and psalms of salvation. The first kind warns the authorities or people in times of complacency; the second encourages them in times of discouragement. These also have certain expected features. Oracles of judgment will typically contain a charge or indictment and the sentence or judgment. (See Amos 1:3-5, 6-8, etc.)

Oracles of salvation will usually include a word of encouragement ("Fear not..."), a motivation for hope and a promise. (See Isa 43:1-8.)

- **Poetry**: Biblical poetry has a distinct format, called parallelism, that is easy to recognize. Simply put, the poet says something, and then says it again using different words. In the Bible these are usually formatted into verse lines, with the first line capitalized and the second line indented. Poetic parallelism is a flexible medium and is sometimes used to pair stanzas as well as lines, or in other combinations. Three kinds of parallelism are usually recognized:
  - **symmetrical parallelism**, the basic form which repeats the thought and often the grammar; an alternative form. This is the pattern in most psalms, which can be seen to pile up sentiments of praise. See Psalm 2.
  - **antithetical parallelism**, that uses contrast of expression to repeat the same thought. Antithetical parallelism is characteristic of proverbial literature. See, for instance, Proverbs 10.
  - **synthetic parallelism**, which doesn't actually repeat. It can be recognized in the way the second line continues the thought, rather than repeating it as in parallelism proper. Synthetic parallelism is often used to break up the relentless pattern of repetition, and can be found in any biblical poetry. See Ps 1:1.

- **History**: Historical writing in the Bible should not be confused with the scientific, critical manner of writing history we have today. History writing in the Bible and other documents in ancient times prized stories as much as reports, legends as much as documentation. When the biblical writers tell the story of their world, notice how the character of the narrative can change from one passage to another, from one book to another. Compare, for instance, the different stories in the book of Judges and the accounts of the various kings, in 1 and 2 Kings.

- **Proverbs and Wisdom Writing**: Proverbs and other wisdom writings are philosophical in a general and nontechnical way. Often it may not be explicitly religious. As with other biblical poetry, Proverbs uses poetic parallelism. Conventional wisdom writing considers that which constitutes the successful life. Its opinions are often pragmatic and conventional. Some wisdom books—Job and Ecclesiastes—radically question the commonplace observations of standard wisdom books.

- **Law Code**: The Old Testament contains three major collections of laws—Exodus 20-23; Leviticus 1-27; Deuteronomy 5-26. These contain a mixture of religious and civil laws. The law codes are connected to the Moses covenant between God and the people Israel, and they can properly be understood as representing the people's side of the covenant agreement. Although they are associated with Moses, the law codes display differences among themselves, and give indication of having grown over time, adapting to different circumstances.

Some examples of New Testament forms:

- **Gospel**: The New Testament Gospels tell the story of Jesus from his baptism to his resurrection. Two of them, Matthew and Luke, introduce their narrative with an account of Jesus' birth. John introduces his narrative with a poetic prologue. The Gospels interpret the meaning of Jesus by the way they tell the story. The common understanding among biblical scholars is that Mark composed his gospel around 70 a.d., constructing it from stories and sayings of Jesus that had been preserved. Most exegetes hold that Matthew and Luke based their writing on Mark's Gospel, along with other sources. John was clearly doing something else.

- **Letter**: The letters of Paul typically follow a certain pattern, beginning with an introductory greeting and a section called the thanksgiving and ending with concluding blessings and greetings. In between, a doctrinal section is followed by a moral section. Some letters, such as I Corinthians, break this pattern. Other letters are attributed to Peter, John, Jude, and James.

- **Parable**: Parables have been described as narrative metaphors. If a metaphor is an image used in a comparison, a parable is a story that is used in a comparison. A common classification of parables would divide them between **similitudes**, which draw a lesson from a common occurrence (such as the Sower parable, Mark 4:1-9), and **narrative parables**, which tell a once-upon-a-time story (such as the Good Samaritan, Luke 10:30-37, or the Prodigal Son, Luke 15:11-32).

- **Apocalyptic**: Apocalyptic writing, which appears in the Old Testament (Daniel) and the New Testament (Revelation) is a kind of writing that interprets the time of the author in elaborate images. It is characterized by dualistic thought (a good power and an evil power), major struggles, and natural cataclysms. It might be considered a literature of consolation to a people who are subject to decisions made elsewhere beyond their control.

- **Miracle Story**: The gospels contain different stories which have their own typical forms. This is probably due to the origin of these stories in the oral tradition remembering Jesus, which when written down became the sources for the Gospel writers. Oral tradition favors this kind of patterned accounts. One of these forms is the miracle story of healing. A typical pattern in a healing miracle story is (a) introduction to a sufferer, sometimes with a description of the illness, (b) encounter with Jesus, with an account of the meeting and usually a dialogue between Jesus and the other party, (c) a description of the healing action, (d) proof of the success of the healing, and, frequently (e) an account of the crowd response. To view some examples see Mark 1-3.

For further exploration:

> The Reading Guides of the *Catholic Study Bible* identifies the literary form of the different biblical books, and often of smaller forms within the books.

Ch. 6. What is strange? *Special words and terms*

One frequent difficulty in reading the Bible is encountering unfamiliar names of persons or places. And sometimes what seems familiar is much stranger than we realize.

Questions to ask:

What proper nouns are included in the passage?
If some are unfamiliar, does the Bible have explanatory footnotes?
How can we use the Reading Guides to help?

What geographical sites are mentioned?
How does locating these in the maps of your Bible help to make sense of the passage?

What "biblical" language is found in the passage (e.g., "righteous")?
Can this language be defined or paraphrased from the context of the passage?
How can the Glossary in the Study Bible help?

* **Place names**:

Unfamiliar place names may cause confusion. For instance the Bible speaks of "Assyria" as well as "Syria." But these are different places. In addition, Syria may be going under the name of "Aram" in the particular time of that writing. Again, the name "Zion" appears frequently in poetry as another name for Jerusalem. It is properly the name of the temple hill. But we know that poetry requires saying things twice using different words. Zion serves that purpose for Jerusalem

Some place names may seem familiar but hide further meanings. "Jerusalem" is a city, of course, which you can visit today in pilgrimage tours. However, it has many different meanings, often referring to its people—the actual inhabitants or even an ideal society. See, for instance, Isaiah 40:2; Galatians 4:25-26; Revelation 21:1-13.

* **Names of Persons**:

The names of persons can be difficult in their own right. But when they are used to indicate entire populations, it can really get confusing. Here are some examples of the way names are used and what some of them mean. There are, of course, many more than those listed here.

* **Joseph**: In Amos 6:6 the prophet speaks of the ruin of Joseph. Your Bible may or may not explain in a footnote that this refers to the inhabitants of the northern kingdom of Israel. It was settled by the Joseph tribes, Ephraim and Manasseh, and so Amos uses the name of the ancestor to indicate the entire people. This kind of usage is not uncommon in the Bible.

* **Herod**: Herod the Great is the person that we often think about when this name appears in our readings. However, in many cases it is not this Herod that is meant,

but one of his descendants. For instance: Matthew 2:3 (Herod the Great); Mark 6:14 (Herod Antipas, son of Herod the Great); Acts 25:13 (Herod Agrippa, great-grandson of Herod the Great).

- **Daniel**: His name means something like "God is judge." Biblical names often have the particle "el" in them. This is a version of "Elohim," the Hebrew word for God. Other names often begin with "Jo-" or end with "-iah." These are versions of "Yahweh," God's name in the Bible. Most Hebrew names are complete sentences. For instance, "Michael" is a rhetorical question: "Who is like God?" (The proper answer is: "No one.") Other such names: Joseph, Elijah, Joel, Gabriel, Israel.

- **LORD**: Often the Bible will have the title "Lord" in all capital letters. This is a reference to the name "Yahweh." Following Jewish traditions of deference, where the name of God was substituted by the title Lord, when reading the Bible, English translations make this substitution. It is in all capitals for two reasons: (1) to distinguish it from the actual word "Lord," which also is used of God in Hebrew tradition, and (2) to imitate the "tetragrammaton" ("four letters"), YHWH, which reflects the Hebrew word—a language in which the vowels are not written out.

For further exploration:

The *Catholic Study Bible*, as with many Bibles, includes a **Glossary** in the back. Here you can find short explanations of terms frequently encountered in reading the Bible. Note also the selective **Concordance**, which will take you to the more important passages, listed by content or theme.

Ch. 7. Who is speaking in the passage? *Implied voices and hearers*

Here we are concerned with the voices implied in the text, and not the actual human author. Note that biblical writing doesn't always use quotation marks to indicate speakers.

Questions to ask:

Which part of the text is a narrator's voice, and which part is the narrator quoting another speaker?
What would be a typical example of such a speaker or voice?

Are some speakers quoting other speakers?
Is there more than one implied speaker?

What would be an example of the type of audience intended by this writing?
How does the text show these things?

- **Author**: The person who produced the text we are reading, whether it is a contemporary writing or ancient writing. Among these would be the human authors of the Bible. We might say that the author lives (and dies) outside the text. And while there may be hints about that person in the writing, we know that the author lives a life, going about his or her business, separate from the text. For instance, F. Scott Fitzgerald was the writer of *The Great Gatsby*. Someone we call "Mark" was the author of a Gospel.

- **Narrator**: The narrator is a name we give the primary voice in a text. This voice in the text telling the story is separate from the author. The narrator is inside the text, present every time we pick up the book, while the author is outside the text. Careful writers consider the kind of narrative voice they want to tell the story. For instance, Nick Carraway, a character in the novel, is the narrating voice of The Great Gatsby. Some narrators are "omniscient," meaning that they can relate what occurs in the inner life of persons in the narrative. Mark's narrator is omniscient.

- **Other voices**: While the narrator tells the story, persons in the story speak up. These too are under the control of the author, and merit our attention. All speeches in quotation marks are other voices. Often the Bible, as in the prophetic books, doesn't use quotation marks, and so the reader must pay close attention.

- **Implied Audience**: In addition to the voices in the text, we can detect what kind of listener is implied by the writing. Being alert to this side of written literature aids our understanding of its message. For instance, action stories would imply male readers; romance novels would imply female readers. While in actuality this may not be the case, the text itself would suggest this situation.

Example: Isa 43:16-21 (see ch. 4, above)

We have looked at this passage in terms of its images of Exodus and return from Exile. Now we can see that the two parts of the passage involve different speakers. In the first part we have a narrative voice (to be distinguished from the author), while in the second part the Lord speaks.

Why distinguish between the prophet and the narrative voice? Certainly the narrator speaks in the prophet's name, but we should be aware that the narrator is a voice created by the author to achieve certain effects. (Furthermore, the prophet as "author" is responsible for *all* of the passage.)

Another way to make this point is to use an analogy from our own experience: the guest speaker at a banquet. In the introductory part of this passage we have the emcee's introduction of the speaker, providing a short bio of past accomplishments. In the second part, the guest speaker himself (Yahweh) addresses the audience.

For further exploration:

In addition to the narrative voice in the text, critics also speak of the **implied author**. The implied author is simply the author as implied by the text, and is to be distinguished from the real author, about whom we have information from other sources than the text itself. Strictly speaking, "Mark," as author of a Gospel, is the implied author. We do not have information about the actual person, apart from the written Gospel itself.

Similarly, the implied author is to be distinguished from the narrator (or narrative voice). The narrative voice is the voice in the text that is telling the story. The implied author is the writer (not the voice) insofar as the text itself tells us about the person writing it.

To be complete, each of these—real author, implied author, and narrator—presupposes a receiver of some kind: the real reader, the implied reader, and the narrator's listener. Not all of these are equally useful for interpreting writing. Nonetheless, the **implied reader**, for instance, helps us understand for whom the writing was originally intended.

Part II. Context and background: The World-Behind-the-Text

Behind the text is the writer as well as the community that brought the text forth. We can think of the writing in front of us as one part of a conversation between the writer and the writer's community. We can safely assume that texts were produced in response to a situation that the writer felt needed addressing. One of the objectives of the informed reader is to work out the situation—the problem, if you will—that called forth the text.

Similarly, there is a location on this side of the text, consisting of you and me, the readers. Just as in the world behind the text, so in a the world in front of the text we have a community of believers—those addressed by the text. Our relationship to the text is, in a way, that of eavesdroppers (For instance, Paul's letters were addressed to communities such as Philippians and Romans, not to us). And yet these writings have entered the canon of sacred scripture, which means, for one thing, that they have meaning for us as well. Though one aspect of informed reading is to understand as clearly as we can the meaning in these writings in their original setting, another aspect is to bring that meaning home to where we reside, here and now. In this section we look at both of these aspects.

Ch. 8. What do the experts say? *The commentaries and study guides*

Why we waited to consult the experts: The main reason for delaying the moment in which we consult the experts is to make room for our own encounter with the biblical texts. Looking up the meaning first can short-circuit this process. Once we have done some reading on our own, we have some ideas we can confirm, and some questions that we can hope to clear up.

Questions to ask:

Gather your findings.
Compare them with an accepted commentary (either biblical or lectionary).
What is the main thing that you find?

Where does the commentary differ from your own findings?
What does the commentary clear up?

What among your findings does the commentary neglect to mention?
What in the commentary makes sense because of your earlier study?

The Catholic Study Bible as learning tool: This Bible is a splendid resource when we know how to use it. Look in the front and back for extra helps that the editors have offered. In addition, this edition of the Bible has Reading Guides, which are equivalent to an introductory text book for the Bible.

Other items with which you might become familiar:
The footnote systems. There are two—one for cross-references to other parts of the Bible; one which is explanatory for difficult passages.

At the back: Glossary. Concordance. Lectionary charts. Maps.

For further exploration:

Many kinds of extra-biblical aids are published for study:

- **Commentaries**: These books are devoted to interpreting individual books of the Bible. Each biblical book is commented upon by a different scholar. Usually they are published as stand-alone volumes. Sometimes, however, they are gathered into one or two volumes.

- **Bible Dictionaries**: These study tools explain different biblical topics, which are arranged in alphabetical order. They are more like encyclopedias than dictionaries.

- **Liturgical commentaries**: Many Catholic periodical publications offer a column on the Sunday scripture readings. These typically apply the scripture to the liturgical occasion.

- **Concordances**: A concordance shows where words or passages in the Bible can be found. A complete concordance will list every word in the Bible (except the most common) in alphabetic order. Under each word a list of verses in biblical order will show where the word is to be found.

- **Gospel Parallels**: A handy tool for Gospel study is a book of parallels. These usually concern the "Synoptic Gospels"—Matthew, Mark, and Luke. Their procedure is to align in three columns the various Gospel stories in order, as a method of allowing comparison among the different versions.

- **Online Aids**: These days there a number of online aids that are useful. For example, Bible Gateway (http://www.Biblegateway.com/) offers a search function that works like a Concordance, only cheaper and quicker.

- **Bible Atlases**: These address the geographical issues of reading the Bible with a collection of maps, usually arranged chronologically from Old Testament historical periods through the New Testament era. While there are only a few geographical areas involved, they change names, political borders, and populations through the centuries of Biblical history. Bible atlases help to tell the story through time.

Ch. 9. What historical information do we need to know? *Historical background*

We often speak of reading the Bible in context. An important part of the context is its historical setting. There are two ways of thinking about the historical dimension of biblical writing. On the one hand, there are the events that the authors write about. This account of events is mysterious to us today without studying it. On the other hand, there is the historical time of the writing and the author's historical setting. For instance, when an author is writing history, he or she is writing long after the events being discussed. And yet there may be a reason to discuss them at that time.

Questions to ask:

What do we know about the biblical book from which this passage was selected?

If an Old Testament text, do we know in what era is as written?
What were the issues that predominated at this time?

If it is a New Testament text, is it a narrative or a letter?
If it is a narrative, can we place the passage in its larger context?
If it is a letter, what prompted its writing?
Can we determine this passage's function within the larger letter?

What follows below is a brief introduction to some of the main lines of the historical background to the biblical books. For a more complete introduction, consult one of the many biblical introductions that are available, beginning with the Reading Guides in the *Catholic Study Bible*.

Old Testament history (*as the Old Testament tells it*):

Ancient historians did not approach the task of writing history in the way modern do. Today we have the benefit of many scientific modes of investigating the past; but in ancient times they were just beginning to develop the practice of historical writing. Their notion of history is often closer to our practice of telling family stories. For a fuller treatment of this topic, consult the Reading Guides of the *Catholic Study Bible*.

The Old Testament story can be generally divided into three periods, reflected in the genealogy at the beginning of Matthew's Gospel. Following *Understanding the Old Testament* by Bernhard Anderson, these can be conveniently symbolized by (a) the stone tablets of the covenant; (b) the star of David; and (c) the Menorah, or seven-branched candlestick.

- **The Tablets**: The early period of the patriarchs, Moses, and the tribal league. The book of Genesis quickly takes us through the primeval history and the stories of the patriarchs, Abraham, Isaac, Jacob, and Joseph, many centuries earlier. The bulk of the accounts, however, concern Moses and the generation after him. Accounts are found in Exodus, Leviticus, Numbers, Deuteronomy, Joshua, and Judges.

- **The Star of David**: The period of the Kingdoms begins around 1000 BC. After an early failed effort by Saul, the kingdom is fully established under David, who reigns over all twelve tribal territories in one kingdom. The one kingdom continues under his son and successor, Solomon, but after this the tribal territories separate into two kingdoms, with the ten tribal holdings to the north in a kingdom with the name of "Israel," (922–721 BC) and another to the south, with Jerusalem as its capital, known as "Judah" (922–587 BC).

- **The Menorah**: The time of the exile and afterward begins with the destruction of Jerusalem and its temple. The time of exile in Babylon (587–539 BC) ends with the defeat of Babylon by Cyrus the Great, of Persia. The Persians allow the Judeans to return and rebuild, but they are not allowed to return to an independent kingdom. As a colony under Persian control they now take the form of a religious community. In 332 BC, the Persians are succeeded by the Hellenists (Greeks), when Alexander the Great passes through this area. In 165 BC the Maccabees overturn the Hellenists and inaugurate a century of independent rule. In 63 BC, Pompey the Great enters Jerusalem, and the time of Roman occupation begins.

For further exploration:

Introductory texts for the Old Testament will treat the history of Old Testament times more extensively and completely, from a contemporary point of view. Also, the Reading Guides of the *Catholic Study Bible* devote some pages to this topic.

Old Testament Themes:

Covenant themes offer a useful way to sketch the theological perspectives of the Old Testament. It is important to realize, however, that this religious view is not divorced from political reality, as in the modern worldview.

Covenants were legal agreements that were adapted in the Bible for religious purposes. Scholars distinguish two models of covenant.

- Covenants between God and individuals are seen with Abraham (Genesis 15; 17) and David (2 Samuel 7:11-16). In this model, the stipulations on God's side of the agreement were spelled out. These came to be known as the "promises" to Abraham, and to David. Because God keeps his promises, this covenant model was seen as unconditional. That is, in difficult times it could provide a word of hope.

- The second model, based on political treaties, is seen in the Moses covenant. Here the agreement is between God and the people Israel, with Moses as the negotiator. In this model, the stipulations on Israel's side of the agreement are spelled out, in the Law Codes in Exodus, Leviticus, and Deuteronomy (see ch. 5, above). These came to be known as the "commandments." This covenant model was seen as conditional, in contrast to the previous. In complacent times it provided a word of warning.

Later biblical books, especially the prophetic writings, frequently cite the covenants, although indirectly, alluding to their motifs. Here is brief list of these:

- Abraham covenant motifs: promise of many descendants, of a land, blessing in the name of Abraham (Gen 12; 15; 17).
- David covenant motifs: the king will be God's son, he will have dominion, the dynasty will rule forever. Also, the motif of the "rod," variously treated (2 Sam 7:11-16; see Pss 2; 110; Isa 9:1-6).
- Moses covenant motifs: the conditional note ("if ..."); concern for the vulnerable members of the society—the widow and orphan, stranger in the land, poor person (Ex 22:20-22; see Jer 7:1-15).

New Testament history:

Historical writing in the New Testament primarily concerns the book of Acts of the Apostles. Here we find interpretive features common to ancient historical writing. Note, for instance, the difference between Paul's own account of his time in Damascus and that given by Luke.

The New Testament period is significantly briefer than that of the Old Testament, and can be more usefully treated by way of a short timeline.

BC

332	Alexander the Great in Judea
167	Maccabean revolt
164	Rededication of the Temple (Hanukkah)
142-63	Hasmonean rule; independence
63	Pompey the Great takes Jerusalem for Rome
37	Herod the Great becomes king under Rome
4	Death of Herod the Great

AD

c. 30	Crucifixion of Jesus
45-56	Paul's ministry
67	Traditional date of Peter and Paul
66-70	Jewish War
65-70	Gospel of Mark
80-85	Gospel of Matthew
80-90	Luke-Acts
90-100	John

New Testament Themes:

Two themes important to the Gospels refer to Jesus of Nazareth as Messiah and Servant. Each has Old Testament origins.

- The **Messiah theme** originates with the promise to David, that his house would rule forever. After the loss of the kingdom in 587 B.C., the house of David was lost to history. The biblical texts that were related to it were now reinterpreted to refer to a final culminating return of the kingdom, with the "Anointed One" (Messiah, Christ), or David king, ruling it. The New Testament sees Jesus as fulfilling the promise of the Messiah. One of the tasks of the New Testament is to explain why Jesus does not fit the expectation of the powerful political Messiah.

- The **Servant theme** derives from four passages in Second Isaiah, the "songs of the Suffering Servant" (Isa 42:1-4; 49:1-7; 50:4-11; 52:13—53:12). The identity of this figure is disputed, but it likely refers to the faithful exiled Israelites, treated as a single individual ("corporate personality"). Jesus is also seen as the fulfillment of the prophecies of the Servant. It helps to explain the discrepancy with the Messianic expectations. See, for instance, the Baptism voice in Mark 1:11, where the two themes are combined in a preview of Jesus' story.

Themes important to Paul, as well as the Gospels, include that of the Cross and Resurrection, as well as Faith.

- **Cross**: Jesus died by crucifixion, a manner of execution reserved for lower-class criminals. The gospels strive to show that such a death does not preclude the fact that this is one whom God favors, the Son of God (Matt 27:54). Paul puts the cross at the center of his theology (Gal 6:14), as the sign of God's complete incarnation, to the very limits of human experience (Phil 2:8). As such it becomes something of a criterion of truth.

- **Resurrection**: As the Acts of the Apostles shows (Acts 1:22), witness to the Resurrection of Jesus is at the heart of the New Testament. The apostles' witness reaches into subsequent generations by way of the written word. For Paul, this is the sign of the coming of the new creation, and the very turning of the age (Rom 4:25).

- **Faith**: For Paul, Faith is a commitment of the entire person. It consists in a full trust in God for one's security, more enduring than the temporal crutches we usually depend upon for our security (Rom 3:28; Gal 2:16).

Some Primary formative events:

The destruction of the first and second temples were crucial events important for the self-understanding of the believing communities, and also for the writings of the Bible, written largely in the aftermath of these two events.

The Babylonian destruction of Jerusalem and Solomon's Temple (587 B.C.) followed by the Exile precipitated a faith crisis for Israel. Wrenched from their homeland they were forced to consider themes of suffering and God's absence, monotheism and mission. Upon their return to the land, they were stimulated to collect their writings, memories, and reflections. The Pentateuch established at this time was the beginning of the Bible.

The Roman destruction of the Second Temple (70 A.D.) caused a major divide in Jewish history. For Judaism proper it meant the beginning of rabbinic Judaism as the norm. Most of the New Testament was written in its aftermath, as the Jesus movement gradually distinguished itself from Judaism.

For further exploration:

Beyond the valuable information contained in the Reading Guides of the Study Bible, numerous introductory textbooks are available for exploring the Bible more closely. An inexpensive and well-received, though somewhat dated volume for the Old Testament is Lawrence Boadt's *Reading the Old Testament*. For a more current introduction, see David Carr and Colleen Conway,

Tip: In learning where things are in the Bible, a helpful practice is to make brief outlines of the primary biblical books. These should make sense to you personally. Not only is this a useful way of gaining some control over the shape and contents of the Bible, but you begin to get an idea where certain topics are treated.

Brief outlines can more easily be remembered—two to five sections at best. Do not be concerned about verse numbers; memorize the chapter numbers. For example, outlining the book of Genesis:

Gen 1-11	Proto-history
Gen 12-25	Abraham
Gen 25-36	Jacob
Gen 37-50	Joseph

Note that chapter 25 in the above outline is both the end of the section on Abraham and the beginning of the section on Jacob. Chapter numbers are sufficient to get us to the right page.

Ch. 10. Why was the passage written? *The social location of the writer*

While this chapter sounds similar to the previous, it is different. Rather than the broad strokes of historical eras, this concerns the more specific and narrow circumstances that pushed the author to a response. Instead of focusing on the events that the writer is describing, it focuses on the social and historical context of the writer, at the time of the writing.

Questions to ask:

What do we know about the writer?
Can you determine when the writer lived?

How does this knowledge contribute to an understanding of the motive for writing?
How does the general motive include this particular passage?

How can we surmise from the text itself what issues or problems it was intended to respond to?
How does it go about solving the problem?
What features of the text reflect these conclusions?

The reason for the writing can be seen as the question to which the writing serves as the answer. We begin by looking at the passage itself and thinking of it as a response to a situation or problem that needed to be addressed.

If you have ever been in the situation in which someone with whom you are visiting receives a phone call, requiring you to stand by for the duration. Meanwhile, you try to reconstruct the other end of the conversation by listening to this end. That is something like what we are doing here. We are hearing one end of a conversation between the writer and another (or community of others), whom we know only by inference. But that still allows a considerable amount of information.

Examples of texts informed by knowing their circumstances:

Paul: Philemon 9-10,12,17 (23 Ord C)

- Helpful information about the particular circumstance: Paul returned a slave to his owner, Philemon, at whose house the Christians meet in Colossae. The slave, Onesimus, ran away to Paul, who was in prison, and became a Christian.

- Helpful general background information: The harsh Roman laws on punishing runaway slaves included removing a finger or an eye; even death. The probable locations of Paul and Philemon, with the former in Ephesus and the latter in Colossae. A look on the map shows how close these are, which would allow the runaway slave to go to the nearest large city.

Isaiah: Isaiah 7:10-14 (4 Adv A)

- Helpful information about the particular circumstance: The passage refers obliquely to events concerning king Ahaz and the prophet Isaiah. Ahaz is rejecting advice from Isaiah on the pretense of not wanting to make presumptuous demands on ("tempt") God. Isaiah responds by promising an authentic and more obedient king to replace Ahaz.

- Helpful general background information: Assyria is beginning to develop a major empire. In response, the kings of Damascus and Samaria propose to form a defensive coalition, and invite Jotham, king of Jerusalem, who rejects their offer. When the two kings place Jerusalem under siege, in response to this rejection, vowing to replace Jotham with one of their own (and thereby ending the line of David kings), Jotham suddenly dies, and his young son, Ahaz takes the throne. Against the advice of Isaiah, who reminds Ahaz of God's promise to David (2 Sam 7:11-16), Ahaz decides to appeal to Assyria against the enemies at the door. Unfortunately, Tiglath-Pileser II of Assyria is only too happy to comply. He invades, warning the kings, and stripping Israel of the territory that one day will be Galilee. This is the beginning of the decline and fall of Israel.

Matthew: Matthew 25:1-13 (32 Ord A)

- Helpful general background information: Matthew is writing his Gospel after the destruction of Jerusalem and its Temple, in 70 A.D. Many thought that this event which ended the world as they knew it would mark the Second Coming of Christ. This did not happen, and Matthew addresses this problem with the "delay" of the Bridegroom.

- Helpful information about the particular circumstance? Sometimes this is not available, though commentators can make reasonable surmises.

For further exploration:
As an ongoing project, a good idea is to increase gradually our knowledge of biblical authors and their times.

Short list of biblical writers to learn about (beginning with the Reading Guides):

OT:	NT:	
The Yahwist	Matthew	*look for:*
the Deuteronomist	Mark	their work, their biography
Amos	Luke	their time and circumstances
Isaiah	John	that which is distinctive about their writing
Second-Isaiah	Paul	
Jeremiah		

Ch. 11. Who is being quoted? *Using cross-references*

The New Testament alludes to and quotes the Old Testament extensively. This is understandable once you remember that at this time there was as yet no New Testament. When it was in the process of development, what we call the Old Testament was for them the only Bible. For the New Testament community it was the record of God's will realized in history, and for them it would seem obvious to cite it in support of the message concerning Jesus of Nazareth.

Using the lectionary as a method of Bible study, as we do here, allows a unique approach to the New Testament's use of Scripture. Since the readings from the Old Testament are chosen to align with the Gospel readings, simply by reviewing them on a weekly basis we are involved in thinking about their relationship.

Questions to ask:

Working with the lectionary selections, determine what connections hold between the Gospel and the Old Testament reading.
Are they suggested by the Gospel writer or by the editors of the lectionary?
How can you tell?

Although the New Testament reading in the lectionary usually follows its own seasonal sequence, it has a broad relationship with the other two readings.
What connections do you see?

Turning from the lectionary to the Bible itself, what cross-references do you find in the passages for the day?
What does this add?

- Bible quoting itself: Perhaps the most common instance of the Bible quoting itself is the New Testament quoting the Old. However, the Old Testament writers also quote other Old Testament writers. Without our system of reference by chapter and verse, the writers quoted key lines from a scripture passage they wished to bring into play. This should be understood as referring to the entire passage, and not the quoted line alone. As in other examples of literary allusions, the allusion brings an added dimension to bear upon the passage at hand.

- Using the lectionary as a tool for learning about cross-references: Because the lectionary is thematically arranged, we have a predetermined set of texts. These are connected in a variety of ways, as indicated in the seven ways listed below. But the most significant difference for the purpose of Bible study is that of the general relationship between Old Testament and Gospel readings, on the one hand, in which the lectionary editors drew upon the pool of biblical themes, and the more specific linkage that derives from the biblical author's own design, on the other.

Some things to look for, with examples:

1—**thematic continuity**: The texts share common themes, but have no other apparent connections. Here we can assume that the editorial committee that designed the Sunday Lectionary are drawing upon biblical themes to find a match between the Old Testament and Gospel readings.

> 5 Lent A: Ezekiel 37; Jn 11 - Both the dry bones of a "dead" people and Jesus' friend, Lazarus, emerge from the grave.

2—**key linking phrases, terms**: Often cross-references are artful and subtle, as when later texts (typically Gospels) use terms from earlier texts. In these cases we can assume the references are intended by the biblical writer. This takes us beyond the lectionary editors to the Bible itself.

> 23 Ord B: Isa 35; Mk 7— In describing the deaf-mute's "speech impediment," Mark uses a term from Isaiah 35.
>
> 27 Ord A: Isa 5; Mt 21 — In the vineyard stories of Isaiah and Matthew there are many common terms—building a tower, etc.—suggesting a deliberate allusion.

3—**key images**: Often images connect the readings in interesting ways. Sometimes these might be attributed to the biblical writer, but usually they are testimony to the artfulness of the lectionary editors.

> 24 Ord C: The Golden Calf of Sinai finds an echo in the Fatted Calf of the Prodigal Son parable.
>
> 3 Lent C: The burning bush on Sinai and the withered fig tree offer a contrast between God's call and God's rejection.
>
> 6 Ord A: The bread of Isaiah 58:7 and the salt of Matt 5:13 offer complementary images.
>
> 12 Ord B: The storms of Job's whirlwind and Mark's Sea of Galilee are theophanies, or displays of God's presence.

4—**featured names/persons**: Particular meanings cluster around certain biblical characters, and this can be a cause for pairing them in Lectionary settings. In this case it is not obvious that the biblical writer has the connection in mind. Other indications may show that it is the case, however.

> 4 Adv B: The promises to David (also called the Covenant with David) is cited by Gabriel in his words to Mary. Clearly intended by Luke.
>
> 29 Ord A: Cyrus and Caesar are comparable emperors, at different times.
>
> 3 Ord A: Isa 8; Matt 4 - Here Zebulon and Naphtali are part of a quotation that is obviously intended by Matthew.

5—**direct quotes**: In some cases later texts explicitly quote earlier texts. Here we can assert with some confidence that the Bible is quoting itself.

> 3 Ord A: Isa 8; Matt 4 - Zebulon & Naphthali: seen in the previous example.
>
> 1 Lent C: Deut 26 - The story of Jesus' temptation in the desert repeatedly quotes Deuteronomy, suggesting a general connection with the first reading.
>
> 31 Ord B: Deut 6 (Shema); Great Commandment — Mark shows Jesus citing Deuteronomy.
>
> 29 Ord B: Isa 53 (4th Servant Song); Mk 10:45 — Jesus completes his lessons on Servant discipleship with a rather explicit allusion to the 4th Servant song.

6—**parallel structures**: When two texts are patterned alike, they may or may not be part of author's intent.

> 28 Ord C: Naaman and 10 lepers: The exclusively Lucan account of the 10 lepers, with its themes of foreigners, thanks, and praise, does not directly cite the Naaman story, though there are many similarities. (However, once we consider Luke 4:27, we may wonder if Luke didn't intend such a connection.)
>
> 3 Ord C: Ezra reads the law; Jesus reads in Nazareth synagogue. These two episodes have similar patterns, but no indication of any deliberate allusion.
>
> 2 Ord B: Both Samuel and John effect a second try. While there is no link between the two stories, in each case the narrative features a second effort.

7—**shared or contrasting theology**: In some liturgical examples, the texts expand upon or contrast theological teachings. This may be a consequence of the biblical passage itself, or simply that of the lectionary editors.

> 18 Ord C: Ecclesiastes (riches); Rich Fool (Lk 12)— The common theme is the problem of riches. There is no direct quote linking the two passages, but the Rich Fool's decision to "eat, drink, and be merry" echoes the famous advice from Ecclesiastes (2:24; 5:17; etc.), leading us to speculate on their relationship.
>
> 22 Ord B: Statutes (Dt); Mark 7 (altering Leviticus!) — Deuteronomy endorses statutes, while Jesus rejects some of them.

The Sunday Lectionary links Gospel readings with appropriate readings from the Old Testament. In some cases these represent connections intended by the Gospel writer, who is purposely alluding to or quoting this particular Old Testament passage. In other cases this may be true, but it is difficult to tell. Finally, there are cases in which the two texts share similar biblical concerns, but there is no evidence that the Gospel writer had this particular passage in mind.

Biblical authors did not cite other biblical books just for decorative purposes. This was their artful method of alluding to entire passages (where we might use footnotes). Consider them to be bringing the referenced passage into play in the case they are making. The New Testament authors were Jewish, so we can assume that they would have the original meaning of those texts in mind, but now supporting the story of Jesus and its meaning for them. And now, for us.

Part III. Community of Believers: The World-in-Front-of-the-Text

The social presence: A praiseworthy practice in Bible study circles is to engage in faith sharing. While, as noted earlier, this is not the emphasis in this method, it is worth noting that another difference is that following this model so often we interact with the Bible in an individualistic way. We read texts and ask ourselves how they might influence our personal lives. But there is a major dimension missing in this approach, and that is the communal and social aspect of the engagement. This is true both at our end of the interchange and at the biblical end. We can discuss this in three areas.

Just as there is a world behind the text—the historical community that called the text into existence—so there is a world in front of the text. That is where we, the readers, find ourselves, attempting to discern its meaning. In one sense we have already seen this when we were considering the reasons for involving the Sunday Lectionary as the basis for Bible study. While we can read the Bible for strictly personal benefit, it is crucial to remember that we belong to a worshiping community that gathers around these Scripture passages on any given weekend.

One advantage of maintaining an awareness of the community of believers on this side of the text is that we can then begin to appreciate aspects of the community on the far side of the text, especially the social issues that generate many of the biblical writings. Limiting the biblical reading experience to an engagement with myself as an individual unnecessarily cuts off my awareness of the justice dimension of the Bible.

In Part III we look more directly at the implications of the community of believers as readers of the text. This will be the subject of chapter 12. In addition, there are two chapters on the Lectionary itself. Chapter 13 describes the design of the liturgical seasons. Chapter 14 consists of a series of charts indicating what texts are assigned to the various Sundays of the 3-year cycles.

Ch. 12. Why does it matter? Application; social location of the reader

There are various ways to think about the world in front of the text. One of these is to consider how the Scriptures affect me personally. Another is to consider the world in front of the text in its fuller social presence. At one level this implies that I am reading the Bible as a member of a faith community, and not simply as a believing individual. At another level, here on the near side of the biblical text we find the social reality with its demands of charity and justice that corresponds in many ways to the world that inspired the writing in the first place. It is in asking this kind of question that often we discover the biblical text's own concern for social justice.

Questions to ask:

How do the readings challenge us?
What do I learn about my own situation or social world through the set of readings?

How do the two problem situations, biblical and contemporary, reflect one another?
How do they differ?

How does the writer's response suggest something for ourselves?
What are some lessons for today?

Moving from Bible (there) to life (here). Some biblical perspectives.

- **The biblical world**: The Bible is the product of a community, that of the original Israel and the New Israel, the Christian church. Much of it is anonymously written, compiled, and edited by members of those communities. Most of it is written in light of community concerns and social issues, rather than personal growth. While it is certainly valid to read a passage in service of personal spirituality, it is wise to remember the reasons it was originally written.

- **The liturgical community**: Moving from the world behind the text to the world in front of the text, we find a community here as well. I do not read the Bible as an isolated individual. I read it as one member of a faith community that takes its self-understanding from the biblical word. It is for this reason that this method uses the Sunday lectionary readings for its objects of study. Properly viewed, this worshiping community of which we are a part is the successor of the community that produced the written word of the Bible. Furthermore, it doesn't take much acquaintance with the biblical texts to realize that the early communities shared the same (or very similar) problems that exercise our own.

- **The social reality**: One important consequence of recognizing the public, communal, and social dimension of scripture is a fresh appreciation of its pervasive message of social justice. Without an understanding of this dimension we will find it difficult to advance beyond personal and individual appropriation of the biblical message.

For further exploration:

In recent years new areas of study have emerged in biblical circles. Here are some brief descriptions of more recent biblical perspectives:

- **Historical anthropology**: A recent development in the past few years is the application of anthropological categories to New Testament history. The cultural differences between today and twenty centuries past, between America and the Middle East, can provide cause for misunderstanding. This body of studies examines this area. Themes such as holy and unclean, honor and shame, diadic personality are uncovered in this endeavor. (For an accessible example, see: Bruce Malina, *The New Testament World*.)

- **Empire studies**: This body of studies takes a page from Postcolonial Criticism and applies it to the Bible. Postcolonial Criticism is a relatively recent phenomenon in the academic world, and consists of the critical report from formerly colonized countries (India, Africa, Caribbean, etc.) on the experience of imperialism. Scripture scholars, recognizing that both Old and New Testaments were written under similar circumstances, have productively explored the meaning of imperial pressure on biblical communities and writers. That such pressure is not explicitly stated is part of the evidence, in a way, as writers find less risky ways of making their points. (See John Dominic Crossan and Jonathan Reed, *In Search of Paul*.)

- **Jewish New Testament studies**: Realizing that the destruction of the Jerusalem Temple in 70 A.D. served as the beginning of Rabbinic Judaism as well as Christianity, in recent years a crop of Jewish scholars have made their specialty the study of the New Testament. While it stands as a hostile witness to Judaism, still the New Testament is the earliest witness to those days out of which contemporary Judaism emerged. The readings that this group produces, as outside witnesses, are invariably informing. (See Amy-Jill Levine, *The Misunderstood Jew*.)

- **Liberation Theology,** *one model of social interpretation*: Jon Sobrino's "hermeneutic circle."

  "Hermeneutic" is a name for interpretation, its theory and practice. The classic hermeneutic circle is the back-and-forth alternation of viewing the text as a whole and looking more closely at its parts. This pattern of reading leads to increased understanding, as each perspective builds on the previous.

  Sobrino's version of this circle relates to "liberation theology," and might be summarized as follows:

  1. To begin, let us say that I am a serious and faithful Christian. Perhaps at some point I place my faith in a stressful situation by, let us say, volunteering to work in a poverty-stricken area such as Haiti.
  2. At this point I may have a crisis in my faith understanding, as my comfortable faith stance endures a challenge. At this point I have a choice. I may, as some do, reject my faith. Or I may return to the sources, examining the scripture for closer clues to my predicament.

3. At this juncture I may discover a dimension of biblical justice (or "preferential option for the poor") that I never before suspected, since I had not until now occasion to consider it.
4. This puts me in a new relation to the biblical word and, arguably, in at new level of faith.

(For an attractive explanation of Sobrino's Circle, see Michael Crosby, *The Spirituality of the Beatitudes*.)

Ch. 13. Lectionary: The Seasons

The Sunday Lectionary is at the heart of this method for many reasons. For one, it is the common experience of reading (or hearing) the Bible for many mainline Christians, and most Catholics. In this way the program builds on what we are already doing.

It also evokes the worshiping community that is virtually present in the study group. We are not isolated individuals but rather a faith community. Add to this the feedback effect, insofar as biblical study of the readings beforehand will enrich one's worship experience in the coming Sunday liturgy.

Another value is that the Lectionary is designed to provide a "tour" of the Bible in the course of three years. This is not a complete tour, for admittedly there are some gaps. However, given the limitations imposed by the three-year cycle, it is remarkably representative of the biblical writings.

Unfortunately many of the readings are unnecessarily brief. This may occasion some confusion. However, a study program using the Lectionary can remedy much of this by studying the texts in their context and setting while at the same time allowing interested groups a basis for exploring the full Bible.

The exposition below is a description of the shape and rationale of the Sunday Lectionary:

The Yearly Cycles:

For the most part, the three annual cycles of readings follow the Synoptic Gospels, Matthew, Mark, and Luke. These correspond to Cycles A, B, and C, in turn.

John's Gospel is not ignored. The first part of the Gospel is featured during Lent; the second part during the Easter season. In addition, Each Ordinary Season begins with readings from John 1, and in Cycle B, John's "Bread of Life" discourse (John 6) interrupts the Mark series of readings.

The Ordinary Church Year (that part that does not include the special seasons of Advent, Christmas, Lent, and Easter) follows the progress of the Gospel for the main part. The editors have tried to avoid repetition, so each cycle tends to emphasize what is unique to that particular Gospel. Mark, the first Gospel to be written, is the foundational document for the Synoptic Gospels. In Cycle B the basic story is emphasized. Matthew's Gospel is known for its five major discourses (Matt 5-7, 10, 13, 18, 24-25), and these are featured in Cycle A. Finally, Luke's Gospel is unique for its long central section featuring Jesus' journey to Jerusalem (Luke 9:51—18:15), and this provides much of the material for Cycle C. John's Gospel is known for its extended dramatic stories and long discourses by Jesus. The first of these appear in Lent; the second appears during the Easter season.

The Old Testament readings are aligned with the Gospel. The nature of this connection varies, from a general thematic similarity to very specific references. One of the useful educational moves is to discover the nature of this relationship. The Old Testament covers a lot of ground and in no way can be comprehensively treated in the three year cycle of readings. However, the lectionary does a good job of touching on the high points of the Hebrew Bible, and this method can profitably be used to explore its meaning and contours.

The New Testament readings (Epistles), mostly from the letters of Paul, but not entirely, follow their own seasonal track. While the readings exhibit the usual brevity of selection, all of Paul's letters are covered in the three year cycle, and the method can be used to explore his writings.

The Special Seasons:

The special seasons are constructed differently from the Ordinary Year, and often show the influence of traditional features for these seasons. One constant features is that the readings are chosen for their appropriateness for this particular day, and for the most part do not have a sequential movement through a series of Sundays.

Advent:

The four Sundays of Advent include an Old Testament reading, an Epistle, usually from Paul, and a Gospel reading. A traditional pattern that governs the season is an emphasis on different aspects of "Advent" or "coming" for different Sundays. The first Sunday of Advent features the eschatological Second Coming. The second and third Sundays feature John the Baptist and the "coming" of Jesus into his earthly ministry in Galilee. The fourth Sunday, close to Christmas, focuses on the coming of Jesus at his birth and features Mary, his mother.

The Old Testament readings tell their own story. You will notice that certain prophetic texts are favored in different years. The second reading is usually chosen to fit the particular occasion, with no larger sequential plan governing the selections.

Christmas:

The Christmas readings do not vary from year to year, except for the Gospel reading on the feast of the Holy Family and the Baptism of our Lord, each of which draws its text from the Gospel of that cycle. One reason for this regularity is that only the Gospels of Matthew and Luke have infancy narratives, which restricts possible choices. Also, Luke's story is more appropriate for Christmas, while Matthew's story of the Magi is appropriate for Epiphany. John's poetic Prologue is reserved for Christmas Day.

Lent:

Like Advent, the Lenten season is influenced by certain traditional patterns. In each year, drawing upon the Gospel for that year, the first Sunday features the Temptation in the Desert while the second Sunday features the Transfiguration. The remaining Gospel selections favor the dramatic stories in the first half of John's Gospel. This is particularly true of Cycle A. The second reading is chosen to fit with the season and the day.

The Old Testament readings tend to show a sequential pattern, however, tracing a theological thread through the history of the Old Testament period.

Easter:

The Easter season marks a major departure from the pattern seen in the other seasons. Neither the Old Testament nor the letters of Paul make an appearance during this season. Instead, the first reading is taken from Acts of the Apostles. In general, these selections follow the course of the book of Acts, telling its story in am abbreviated way. Once again, however, a program of study based on the lectionary can flesh out these pieces and lead to a fuller understanding of this fascinating book.

The second reading is taken from other books of the New Testament that do not receive much attention otherwise. For the three cycles these are, in turn, 1 Peter, 1 John, and Revelation. Again, for the most part these follow the course of the book in question, inviting fuller understanding and filling in the missing parts.

The following chapter consists of charts of the readings in terms of biblical book, chapter and verse. The Study Bible contains the same information in an appendix, but these charts are given for the purpose of quick reference, visual comparison, and a way of seeing the patterns of usage. These can be very enlightening.

ADVENT AND CHRISTMAS SEASONS, COMPARED

Cycle A	Cycle B	Cycle C
1. Isaiah 2:1-5 Romans 13:11-14 Matthew 24:37-14	Isa 63:16-17,19; 64:2-7 1 Corinthians 1:3-9 Mark 13:33-37	Jeremiah 33:14-16 1 Thessalonians 3:12--4:2 Luke 21:26-28,34-36
2. Isaiah 11:1-10 Romans 15:4-9 Matthew 3:1-12	Isaiah 10:1-5,9-11 2 Peter 3:8-14 Mark 1:1-8	Baruch 5:1-9 Philippians 1:4-8,8-11 Luke 3:1-6
3. Isaiah 35:1-6,10 James 5:7-10 Matthew 11:2-11	Isaiah 61:1-2. 10-11 1 Thessalonians 5:16-24 John 1:8-8,19-28	Zephaniah 3:14-18 Philippians 4:4-7 Luke 3:10-18
4. Isaiah 7:10-14 Romans 1:1-7 Matthew 1:18-24	2 Samuel 7:1-5, 8-11,16 Romans 16:25-27 Luke 1:26-38	Micah 5:2-5 Hebrews 10:5-10 Luke 1:39-45

Christmas:

[Midnight] Isaiah 9:1-6 Titus 2:11-14 Luke 2:1-14	[Dawn] Isaiah 62:11-12 Titus 3:4-7 Luke 2:15-20	[During the Day] Isaiah 52:7-10 Hebrews 1:1-6 John 1:1-18

Sunday after Christmas   (Holy Family)

Sirach 3:3-7,14-17 Colossians 3:12-21 Matthew 2:13-15,19-23	Sirach 3:2-6,12-14 Colossians 3:12-21 Luke 2:22-40	Sirach 3:2-6,12-14 Colossians 3:12-21 Luke 2:41-62

Octave of Christmas   (Mary Mother of God)

Numbers 6:22-27 Galatians 4:4-7 Luke 2:16-21	Numbers 6:22-27 Galatians 4:4-7 Luke 2:16-21	Numbers 6:22-27 Galatians 4:4-7 Luke 2:16-21

Epiphany   (Sunday after Christmas):

Isaiah 60:1-6 Ephesians 3:2-3, 5-6 Matthew 2:1-12	Isaiah 60:1-6 Ephesians 3:2-3, 5-6 Matthew 2:1-12	Isaiah 60:1-6 Ephesians 3:2-3, 5-6 Matthew 2:1-12

Baptism of the Lord:

Isaiah 42:1-4. 6-7 Acts 10:34-38 Matthew 3:13-17	Isaiah 42:1-4,6-7 Acts 10:34-38 Mark 1:7-11	Isaiah 42:1-4,6-7 Acts 10:34-38 Luke 3:15-16,21-22

Cycle A	Cycle B	Cycle C
1. Genesis 2:7-9: 3:1-7 Romans 5:12-19 Matthew 4:1-11	Genesis 9:8-16 1 Peter 3:18-22 Mark 1:12-15	Deuteronomy 26:4-10 Romans 10:8-13 Luke 4:1-13
2. Genesis 12:1-4 2 Timothy 1:8-10 Matthew 17:1-9	Genesis 22:1-2.9-13.15-18 Romans 8:31-34 Mark 9:2-10	Genesis 15:5-12. 17-18 Philippians 3:17--4:1 Luke 9:28-36
3. Exodus 17:3-7 Romans 5:1-2, 5-8 John 4:5-42	Exodus 20:1-17 1 Corinthians 1:22-25 John 2:13-25	Exodus 3:1-8,13-15 1 Corinthians 10:1-8,10-12 Luke 13:1-9
4. 1 Samuel 16:1,6-7,10-13 Ephesians 5:8-14 John 9:1-41	2 Chron 36:14-17,19-23 Ephesians 2:4-10 John 3:14-21	Joshua 5:9,10-12 2 Corinthians 5:17-21 Luke 15:1-3. 11-32
5. Ezekiel 37:12-14 Romans 8:8-11 John 11:1-45	Jeremiah 31:31-34 Hebrews 5:7-9 John 12:20-33	Isaiah 43:16-21 Philippians 3:8-14 John 8:1-11

Passion Sunday:

Cycle A	Cycle B	Cycle C
Matthew 21:1-11	Mark 11:1-10	Luke 19:28-40
-----------------------------	----------------------------	----------------------------
Isaiah 50:4-7 Philippians 2:6-11 Matthew 26:14—27:66	Isaiah 50:4-7 Philippians 2:6-11 Mark 14:1—15:47	Isaiah 50:4-7 Philippians 2:6-11 Luke 22:14—23:56

EASTER SEASONS, COMPARED

Cycle A	Cycle B	Cycle C
Easter Sunday:		
Acts 10:34,37-43	Acts 4:32-35	Acts 5:12-16
Colossians 3:1-4	Colossians 3:1-4	Colossians 3:1-4
John 20:1-9	John 20:1-9	John 20:1-9
or: Matthew 28:1-10	or: Mark 16:1-8	or: Luke 24:1-12
2. Acts 2:42-47	Acts 4:32-35	Acts 5:12-16
1 Peter 1:3-9	1 John 5:1-6	Revelation 1:9-13,17-19
John 20:19-31	John 20:19-31	John 20:19-31
3. Acts 2:14,22-28	Acts 3:13-15,17-19	Acts 5:27-32,40-41
1 Peter 1:17-21	1 John 2:1-5	Revelation 5:11-14
Luke 24:13-35	Luke 24:35-48	John 21:1-19
4. Acts 2:14,36-41	Acts 4:8-12	Acts 13:14,43-52
1 Peter 2:20-25	1 John 3:1-2	Revelation 7:9,14-17
John 10:1-10	John 10:11-18	John 10:27-30
5. Acts 6:1-7	Acts 9:26-31	Acts 14:21-27
1 Peter 2:4-9	1 John 3:18-24	Revelation 21:1-5
John 14:1-12	John 15:1-8	John 13:31-35
6. Acts 8:5-8,14-17	Acts 10:25-26,34-35,44-48	Acts 15:1-2,21-29
1 Peter 3:15-18	1 John 4:7-10	Revelation 21:10-14,22-23
John 14:15-21	John 15:9-17	John 14:23-29
Ascension:		
Acts 1:1-11	Acts 1:1-11	Acts 1:1-11
Ephesians 1:17-23	Ephesians 1:17-23	Ephesians 1:17-23
Matthew 28:16-20	Mark 16:15-20	Luke 24:46-53
7. Acts 1:12-14	Acts 1:15-17,20-26	Acts 7:55-60
1 Peter 4:13-16	John 4:11-16	Rev 22:12-14,16-17,20
John 17:1-11	John 17:11-19	John 17:20-26
Pentecost:		
Acts 2:1-11	Acts 2:1-11	Acts 2:1-11
1 Corinthians 12:3-7,12-13	1 Corinthians 12:3-7,12-13	1 Corinthians 12:3-7,12-13
John 20:19-23	John 20:19-23	John 20:19-23
Trinity Sunday:		
Exodus 34:4-6,8-9	Deuteronomy 1:32-34,39-40	Proverbs 8:22-31
2 Corinthians 13:11-13	Romans 8:14-17	Romans 5:1-5
John 3:16-18	Matthew 28:16-20	John 16:12-15
Corpus Christi:		
Deuteronomy 8:2-3,14-16	Exodus 24:3-8	Genesis 14:18-20
1 Corinthians 10:16-17	Hebrews 9:11-15	1 Corinthians 11:23-26
John 6:51-58	Mark 14:12-16,22-26	Luke 9:11-17

ORDINARY CHURCH YEAR -- A CYCLE

1.	(Baptism of the Lord, *above*)		
2.	Isaiah 49:3.5-6	1 Corinthians 1:1-3	John 1:29-34
3.	Isaiah 8:23—9:3	1 Corinthians 1:10-13,17	Matthew 4:12-23
4.	Zephaniah 2:3; 3:12-13	1 Corinthians 1:26-31	Matthew 5:1-12
5.	Isaiah 58:7-10	1 Corinthians 2:1-5	Matthew 5:13-16
6.	Sirach 15:16-20	1 Corinthians 2:6-10	Matthew 5:15-37
7.	Leviticus 19:1-2,17-18	1 Corinthians 3:16-23	Matthew 5:38-48
8.	Isaiah 49:14-15	1 Corinthians 4:1-5	Matthew 6:24-34
9.	Deuteronomy 11:18,26-28,32	Romans 3:21-25,28	Matthew 7:21-27
10.	Hosea 6:3-6	Romans 4:18-25	Matthew 9:9-13
11.	Exodus 19:2-6	Romans 5:6-11	Matthew 9:36—10:8
12.	Jeremiah 20:10-13	Romans 5:12-15	Matthew 10:26-33
13.	2 Kings 4:8-11,14-16	Romans 6:3-4,8-11	Matthew 10:37-42
14.	Zechariah 9:9-10	Romans 8:9,11-13	Matthew 11:25-30
15.	Isaiah 55:10-11	Romans 8:18-23	Matthew 13:1-23
16.	Wisdom 12:13,16-19	Romans 8:26-27	Matthew 13:24-43
17.	1 Kings 3:5,7-12	Romans 8:28-30	Matthew 13:44-52
18.	Isaiah 55:1-3	Romans 8:35, 37-39	Matthew 14:13-21
19.	1 Kings 19:9,11-13	Romans 9:1-5	Matthew 14:22-33
20.	Isaiah 56:1,6-7	Romans 11:13-15,29-32	Matthew 15:21-28
21	Isaiah 22:19-23	Romans 11:33-36	Matthew 16:13-20
22.	Jeremiah 20:7-9	Romans 12:1-2	Matthew 16:21-27
23.	Ezekiel 33:7-9	Romans 13:8-10	Matthew 18:15-20
24.	Sirach 27:30—28:7	Romans 14:7-9	Matthew 18:21-35
25.	Isaiah 55:6-9	Philippians 1:20-24,27	Matthew 20:1-16
26.	Ezekiel 18:25-28	Philippians 2:1-11	Matthew 21:28-32
27.	Isaiah 5:1-7	Philippians 4:6-9	Matthew 21:33-43
28.	Isaiah 25:6-10	Philippians 4:12-14,19-20	Matthew 22:1-14
29.	Isaiah 45:1,4-6	1 Thessalonians 1:1-4	Matthew 22:15-21
30.	Exodus 22:20-26	1 Thessalonians 1:5-10	Matthew 22:34-40
31.	Malachi 1:14—2:2,8-10	1 Thessalonians 2:7-9,13	Matthew 23:1-12
32.	Wisdom 6:12-16	1 Thessalonians 4:13-18	Matthew 25:1-13
33.	Prov 31:10-13, 29-10,30-31	1 Thessalonians 5:1-6	Matthew 25:14-30

CHRIST THE KING:

34.	Ezekiel 34:11-12,15-17	1 Corinthians 15:20-26,28	Matthew 25:31-46

ORDINARY CHURCH YEAR -- B CYCLE

1.	(Baptism of the Lord, *above*)		
2.	1 Samuel 3:3-10,19	1 Corinthians 6:13-15,17-20	John 1:35-42
3.	Jonah 3:1-5,10	1 Corinthians 7:29-31	Mark1:14-20
4.	Deuteronomy 18:15-20	1 Corinthians 7:32-35	Mark 1:21-28
5.	Job 7:1-4,8-7	1 Corinthians 9:16-19,22-23	Mark 1:29-39
6.	Leviticus 13:1-2,45-46	1 Corinthians 10:31--11:1	Mark 1:40-45
7.	Isaiah 43:18-19,21-22,24-25	2 Corinthians 1:18-22	Mark 2:1-12
8.	Hosea 2:16,17,21-22	2 Corinthians 3:1-6	Mark 2:18-22
9.	Deuteronomy 5:12-15	2 Corinthians 4:6-11	Mark 2:23—3:6
10.	Genesis 3:9-15	2 Corinthians 4:13—5:1	Mark 3:20-35
11.	Ezekiel 17:22-24	2 Corinthians 5:6-10	Mark 4:26-34
12.	Job 38:1,8-11	2 Corinthians 5:14-17	Mark 4:35-41
13.	Wisdom 1:13-15; 2:23-24	2 Corinthians 8:7,9,13-15	Mark 5:21-43
14.	Ezekiel 2:2-5	2 Corinthians 12:7-10	Mark 6:1-6
15.	Amos 7:12-15	Ephesians 1:3-14	Mark 6:7-13
16.	Jeremiah 23:1-6	Ephesians 2:13-18	Mark 6:30-34
17.	2 Kings 4:42-44	Ephesians 4:1-6	John 6:1-15
18.	Exodus 16:2-4,12-15	Ephesians 4:17,20-24	John 6:24-35
19.	1 Kings 19:4-8	Ephesians 4:3—5:2	John 6:41-51
20.	Proverbs 9:1-6	Ephesians 5:15-20	John 6:51-58
21.	Joshua 24:1-2,15-17,18	Ephesians 5:21-32	John 6:60-69
22.	Deuteronomy 4:1-2,6-8	James 1:17-18,21-22,27	Mark 7:1-8,14-15,21-23
23.	Isaiah 35:4-7	James 2:1-5	Mark 7:31-37
24.	Isaiah 50:5-9	James 2:14-18	Mark 8:27-35
25.	Wisdom 2:12,17-2O	James 3:16—4:3	Mark 9:30-37
26.	Numbers 11:25-29	James 5:1-6	Mark 9:38-43,45,47-48
27.	Genesis 2:18-29	Hebrews 2:9-11	Mark 10:2-16
28.	Wisdom 7:7-11	Hebrews 4:12-13	Mark 10:17-30
29.	Isaiah 53:10-11	Hebrews 4:14-16	Mark 10:35-45
30.	Jeremiah 31:7-9	Hebrews 5:1-6	Mark 10:46-52
31.	Deuteronomy 6:2-6	Hebrews 7:23-28	Mark 12:28-34
32.	1 Kings 17:10-16	Hebrews 9:24-28	Mark 12:38-44
33.	Daniel 12:1-3	Hebrews 10:11-14,18	Mark 13:24-32
CHRIST THE KING:			
34.	Daniel 7:13-14	Revelation 1:5-8	John 18:33-37

ORDINARY CHURCH YEAR -- C CYCLE

1.	(Baptism of the Lord, *above*)		
2.	Isaiah 62:1-5	1 Corinthians 12:4-11	John 2:1-12
3.	Nehemiah 8:2-6,8-10	1 Corinthians 12:12-30	Luke 1:1-4: 4:14-21
4.	Jeremiah 1:4-5,17-19	1 Corinthians 12:31—13:13	Luke 4:21-30
5.	Isaiah 6:1-2,3-8	1 Corinthians 15:1-11	Luke 5:1-11
6.	Jeremiah 17:5-8	1 Corinthians 15:12,16-20	Luke 6:17,20-26
7.	1 Sam 26:2,7-9,12-13,22-23	1 Corinthians 15:45-49	Luke 6:27-38
8.	Sirach 27:5-8	1 Corinthians 15:54-58	Luke 6:39-45
9.	1 Kings 8:41-43	Galatians 1:1-2,6-10	Luke 7:1-10
10.	1 Kings 17:17-24	Galatians 1:11-19	Luke 7:11-17
11.	2 Samuel 12:7-10,13	Galatians 2:16,19-21	Luke 7:36—8:3
12.	Zechariah 12:10-11	Galatians 3:26-29	Luke 9:18-24
13.	1 Kings 19:16,19-21	Galatians 5:1,13-18	Luke 9:51-62
14.	Isaiah 66:10-14	Galatians 6:14-18	Luke 10:1-12,17-20
15.	Deuteronomy 30:10-14	Colossians 1:15-20	Luke 10:25-37
16.	Genesis 18:1-10	Colossians 1:24-28	Luke 10:38-42
17.	Genesis 18: 20-32	Colossians 2:12-14	Luke 11:1-13
18.	Ecclesiastes 1:2; 2:21-23	Colossians 3:1-5,9-11	Luke 12:13-21
19.	Wisdom 18:6-9	Hebrews 11:1-2,8-19	Luke 12:32-48
20.	Jeremiah 38:4-6,8-10	Hebrews 12:1-4	Luke 12:49-53
21.	Isaiah 66:18-21	Hebrews 12:5-7,11-13	Luke 13:22-30
22.	Sirach 3:19-21,30-31	Hebrews 12:18-19,22-24	Luke 14:1,7-14
23.	Wisdom 9:13-19	Philemon 9-10,12-17	Luke 14:25-33
24.	Exodus 32:7-11,13-14	1 Timothy 1:12-17	Luke 15:1-32
25.	Amos 8:4-7	1 Timothy 2:1-8	Luke 16:1-13
26.	Amos 6:l, 4-7	1 Timothy 6:11-16	Luke 16:19-31
27.	Habakkuk 1:2-3; 2:2-4	2 Timothy 1:6-8,13-14	Luke 17:5-10
28.	2 Kings 5:14-17	2 Timothy 2:8-13	Luke 17:11-19
29.	Exodus 17:8-13	2 Timothy 3:14—4:2	Luke 18:1-8
30.	Sirach 35:15-17,20-22	2 Timothy 4:6-8,16-18	Luke 18:9-14
31.	Wisdom 11:23—12:2	2 Thessalonians 1:11—2:2	Luke 19:1-10
32.	2 Maccabees 7:1-2,9-14	2 Thessalonians 2:16—3:5	Luke 20:27-38
33.	Malachi 3:19-20	2 Thessalonians 3:7-12	Luke 21:5-19

CHRIST THE KING:

34.	2 Samuel 5:1-3	Colossians 1:12-20	Luke 23:35-43

APPENDIX 1

Sample Passages with brief analysis

1.   **Isaiah 49:14-15   (8 Ord A)**

Can a mother forget her infant?
Zion said, "The LORD has forsaken me;
my LORD has forgotten me."

Can a mother forget her infant,
be without tenderness for the child of her womb?

Even should she forget,
I will never forget you.

Features that can be observed in this passage:

Question and answer pattern
Poetic parallelism: synthetic, antithetic

----

2.   **Isa 43:16-21**   **(5 Lent C)**

Thus says the LORD,
who opens a way in the sea,
a path in the mighty waters,
Who leads out chariots and horsemen,
a powerful army,
Till they lie prostrate together, never to rise,
snuffed out, quenched like a wick.

Remember not the events of the past,
the things of long ago consider not;
See, I am doing something new!
Now it springs forth, do you not perceive it?
In the wilderness I make a way,
in the wasteland, rivers.
Wild beasts honor me,
jackals and ostriches,
For I put water in the wilderness
and rivers in the wasteland
for my chosen people to drink,
The people whom I formed for myself,
that they might recount my praise.

Features that can be observed in this passage:

Contrast in images: Exodus (sea); return from Babylonian Exile (desert)
Voices: introduction; main speaker (Yahweh)

Isaiah 58:7-10   (5 Ord A)

[**If** you] Share your bread with the hungry,
shelter the oppressed and the homeless;
clothe the naked when you see them,
and do not turn your back on your own.

Then your light shall break forth like the dawn,
and your wound shall quickly be healed;
your vindication shall go before you,
and the glory of the LORD shall be your rear guard.

Then you shall call, and the LORD will answer,
you shall cry for help, and he will say: Here I am!

If you remove from your midst
oppression, false accusation and malicious speech;

if you bestow your bread on the hungry
and satisfy the afflicted;

then light shall rise for you in the darkness,
and the gloom shall become for you like midday.

Features that can be observed in this passage:

    If/then pattern:

IF	THEN
share your bread (2x)	your light shall rise (2x)
works of mercy	the Lord will hear you

    Imagery (bread, light)
    Poetic parallelism

4.   **Exodus 22:20-26   (30 Ord A)**

You shall not oppress or afflict a resident _alien_,
for you were once aliens residing in the land of Egypt.
You shall not wrong any _widow_ or _orphan_.
If ever you wrong them and they **cry out to me**,
I will surely listen to their cry.
My wrath will flare up,
and I will kill you with the sword;
then your own wives will be widows,
and your children orphans.

If you lend money to my people, the _poor_ among you,
you must not be like a money lender;
you must not demand interest from them.
If you take your neighbor's cloak as a pledge,
you shall return it to him before sunset;
for this is his only covering;
it is the cloak for his body.
What will he sleep in?
If he **cries out to me**, I will listen;
for I am compassionate.

Pattern:

The passage above, which can be called "the cry of the poor," shows a repeating pattern in three steps:

1. Do not molest the stranger, widow or orphan
2. If they cry out I will hear them
3. For I am a God of wrath.

1. Do not molest the poor person
2. If he cries out to me, I will hear him.
3. For I am a God of compassion.

The basic structure is a warning against molesting the vulnerable in the land. These are named as the stranger, the widow and orphan, and the poor person. In subsequent prophetic writings these figures become emblematic of the social conditions of the times.

What invites reflection is contrast in the final position, between God's wrath and God's compassion

5.   **Galatians 5:1, 13-18   (13 Ord C)**

For freedom Christ set us free;
so stand firm and do not submit again to the yoke of slavery.

For you were called for freedom, brothers.
But do not use this freedom as an opportunity for the flesh;
rather, serve one another through love.
For the whole law is fulfilled in one statement,
namely, "You shall love your neighbor as yourself."
But if you go on biting and devouring one another,
beware that you are not consumed by one another.
I say, then: live by the Spirit
and you will certainly not gratify the desire of the flesh.
For the flesh has desires against the Spirit,
and the Spirit against the flesh;
these are opposed to each other,
so that you may not do what you want.
But if you are guided by the Spirit,
you are not under the law.

Features that can be observed in this passage:

Oppositional terms:

freedom/slavery

Spirit/flesh

law/love

Spirit/law, etc.

In dealing with oppositional terms, notice which are proper to Paul's thinking, and not simply a part of the language. For instance, here we see the contrast **love/law**, whereas the natural contrast would be **love/hate**. This gives a clue to Paul's thinking.

Some pairs of opposed terms coincide with others (**freedom/slavery** seems very close to **Spirit/flesh**), while others relate in different ways. Watch for how the terms relate.

APPENDIX 2

Lectionary Scripture text examples

(NB: The abbreviations for the Sundays identify them by Number-Season-Cycle. Thus, the first example, 5 Ord A is read as "Fifth Sunday of Ordinary Time, Cycle A."

OT

Isa 58:7-10	5 Ord A	if / then
Sir 15:15-20	6 Ord A	parallelism
Isa 49:14-15	8 Ord A	voice
Isa 55:10-11	15 Ord A	image
Isa 55:1-3	18 Ord A	parallelism, unfamiliar terms
I Kgs 19:9, 11-13	19 Ord A	(gap), form
Isa 56:1, 6-7	20 Ord A	cross, (gap), form
Isa 22:19-23	21 Ord A	(gap), cross-reference
Isa 55:6-9	25 Ord A	parts, voice
Exod 22:20-26	30 Ord A	parts, form
Isa 25:6-10	28 Ord A	image
Isa 5:1-7	27 Ord A	voice, parts, image
Isa 43:16-21	5 Lent C	parts, voice, image
Amos 6:1, 4-7	26 Ord C	parallelism, image, unfamiliar terms
Isa 35:4-7	23 Ord B	cross-reference
Deut 26:4-10	1 Lent C	cross-reference, form (credo)
Deut 6:2-8	31 Ord B	cross-reference, form (shema)
Isa 53:10-11	29 Ord B	cross-reference
2 Kgs 5:14-17	28 Ord C	cross-reference
Neh 8:2-7, 8-10	3 Ord C	cross-reference
1 Sm 3:3-10, 19	2 Ord B	cross-reference
Eccles 1:2; 2:21-23	18 Ord C	cross-reference
Deut 4:1-2, 6-8	22 Ord B	cross-reference
Exod 32:7-11, 13-14	24 Ord C	cross-reference
Exod 3:1-8, 13-15	3 Lent C	cross-reference
Isa 45:1, 4-6	29 Ord A	form, voice

NT

Acts 2:1-11	Pentecost	key words
1 Cor 2:1-5	5 Ord A	parts, repetitions, oppositions
1 Cor 2:6-10	6 Ord A	parts, repetitions, oppositions
1 Cor 4:1-5	8 Ord A	parts
1 Cor 12:3-7, 12-13	Pentecost	key words,(gap)
Gal 5:1, 13-18	13 Ord C	oppositional terms
1 Peter 1:17-21	3 Easter A	if/ then
Phil 2:1-11	26 Ord A	form, parts

Gospel

Mt 5:13-16	5 Ord A	parts, images, cross
Mt 5:15-20	6 Ord A	parts, form
Mt 5:38-48	7 Ord A	cross-reference
Mt 6:	8 Ord A	parts, chiasmus
Mt 21:28-32	26 Ord A	cross-reference
Mk 7:31-37	23 Ord B ·	cross-reference
Mt 21:33-34	27 Ord A	cross-reference

Lk 4:1-13	1 Lent C	cross-reference
Mk 10:35-45	31 Ord B	cross-reference
Lk 17:11-19	28 Ord C	cross-reference
Lk 1:1-4; 4:14-21	3 Ord C	cross-reference
Jn 1:35-42	2 Ord B	cross-reference
Lk 12:13-21	18 Ord C	cross-reference
Mk 7:1-8, 14-15, 21-23	22 Ord B	cross-reference
Lk 15:1-32	24 Ord C	cross-reference
Lk 13:1-9	3 Lent C	cross-reference

Selected Bibliography

Anderson, Bernhard. *Understanding the Old Testament*. 5th edition. Prentice-Hall (2006).

Boadt, Lawrence. *Reading the Old Testament: An Introduction*. Second Edition Updated by Richard Clifford and Daniel Harrington. Paulist Press (Sep 4, 2012).

Carr, David and Colleen Conway. *An Introduction to the Bible: Sacred Texts and Imperial Contexts. Wiley*-Blackwell; 1 edition (March 16, 2010)

Crosby, Michael, OSF. *The Spirituality of the Beatitudes*. Orbis Books; Revised edition (January 1, 2005)

Crossan, John Dominic and Jonathan Reed. *In Search of Paul.* HarperOne (November 1, 2005).

Levine, Amy-Jill. *The Misunderstood Jew*. HarperOne (November 20, 2007)

Malina, Bruce. *The New Testament World*. Westminster John Knox Press; Revised, Expand edition (February 1, 2001)

Schneiders, Sandra. *The Revelatory Text*. Michael Glazier Books; 2 edition (July 1, 1999).

Throckmorton, Burton H. Jr. *Gospel Parallels: A Comparison of the Synoptic Gospels,* Thomas Nelson; 5th Revised edition (December 2, 1992).

www.ingramcontent.com/pod-product-compliance
Lightning Source LLC
LaVergne TN
LVHW081326060426
835511LV00011B/1877